BASTIEN

CHRISTMAS FOR ADULTS

Sacred and Popular Christmas Carols

Jane Smisor Bastien, Lisa Bastien, & Lori Bastien

Preface

One of the joys of learning to play the piano is the ability to share music with your family and friends. Christmas For Adults *is a collection of sacred and popular Christmas classics that have culminated over centuries of musical celebration. We hope you enjoy playing and singing these widely-loved carols for many years to come.*

Sincerely,
Jane Smisor Bastien, Lisa Bastien, and Lori Bastien

This icon is used to indicate on which track of the correlated *Accompaniment Compact Disc* each piece can be found. The circled number inside the icon indicates the particular CD track. Also included is the metronome number at which the accompaniment has been recorded. For those books which are purchased with the *Accompaniment Compact Disc*, the CD is attached inside the back cover. More information about the compact disc may be found on page 2.

(Book plus CD) ISBN 0-8497-7303-2 • (Book only) ISBN 0-8497-7304-0

About the *Accompaniment Compact Disc*

If this copy of *Bastien Christmas For Adults* was purchased with the compact disc, the CD can be found attached inside the back cover of the book. The *Bastien Christmas For Adults Accompaniment Compact Disc* was created to musically enhance student practice sessions and improve understanding of phrasing, balance, rhythm, and pulse. Each piece in *Bastien Christmas For Adults* includes two CD tracks — one at a slower "practice tempo" and one at a faster "goal tempo" — to facilitate a methodical mastery of the songs. This allows students to use the accompaniments **as they learn** each piece, rather than waiting until the particular challenges of a piece have been mastered.

Each piece on the *Accompaniment Compact Disc* is preceded by a two measure count-off. On the first beat of each count-off measure, a metallic triangle "ding" is heard, followed by wooden stick "clicks" on the remaining beats of the measure. Once the music begins, tempo will vary as dictated by the markings in the music, such as a *ritardando*.

Fermatas appear in the introductions of some pieces. For reasons of timing and ease of playing, these fermatas are **not** observed on the *Accompaniment Compact Disc*. When the CD is used, the student should continue in tempo. When the piano part is played alone or with a partner playing the duet accompaniments included with some pieces, the fermatas can be observed.

On each piece, background accompaniment instruments are heard on the left channel of the recording. The student piano part as it appears in the book is demonstrated on the right channel. The duet accompaniment parts are not heard on the CD. On many sound systems, balance between the left and right channels may be changed, either by adjusting a single "left/right balance control," or by adjusting the volume of the left and right speakers individually. These adjustments allow isolation of either the accompaniment instruments or the student piano part, or modification of the blend between the two.

When first learning a piece, it is recommended that students adjust their sound systems so that the left and right channels are equal, or so that the right channel is favored, allowing the student piano part to be heard as clearly as possible. As students become more proficient playing a piece, it is suggested that they try adjusting their systems to favor the left channel, thus making the student piano part on the right channel very soft or completely silent. This will allow students to play the piano over the accompaniment without the added sound of the demonstration piano coming from the CD.

If using an electronic keyboard, it is important that the pitch of the keyboard match the tuning note found on track 1 of the CD. This tuning note is A above middle C. The reference manual of each particular keyboard should provide information on how to make tuning adjustments.

CONTENTS

JOLLY OLD ST. NICHOLAS

Duet Accompaniment

When played as a duet, the student part is played one octave higher.

JOLLY OLD ST. NICHOLAS

Traditional American Carol

Moderato

★ The fermatas found here and in other songs are not observed on the *Accompaniment Compact Disc*.

O COME, LITTLE CHILDREN

Duet Accompaniment

When played as a duet, the student part is played one octave higher.

O COME, LITTLE CHILDREN

Music by J. A. P. Schulz
Words by Christoph von Schmid,
Adapted by James Bastien

Moderately

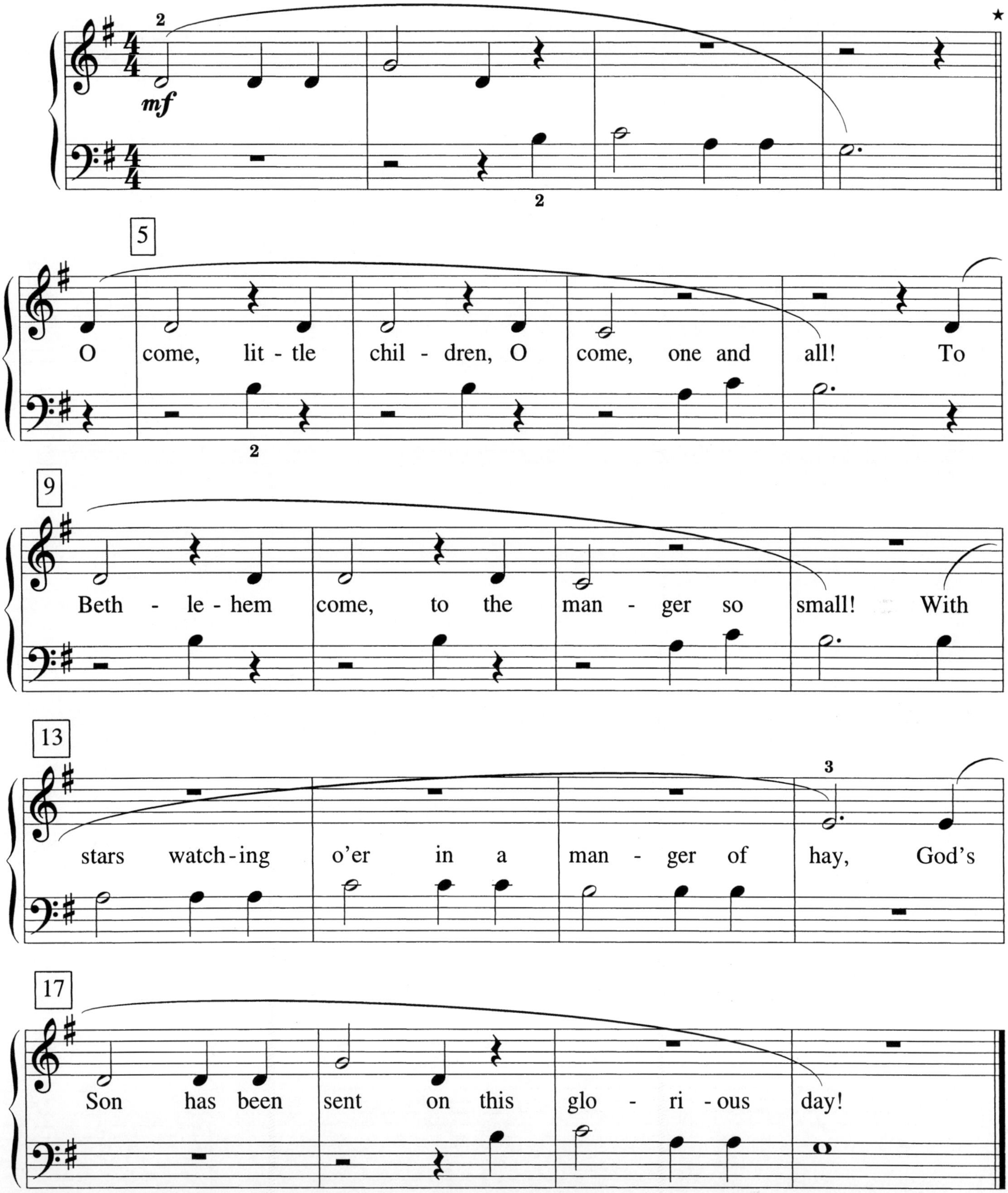

★ A thin double bar line can be used to show the end of a musical section. The end of a section can occur in the middle of a measure, as it does here.

WE WISH YOU A MERRY CHRISTMAS

Duet Accompaniment

When played as a duet, the student part is played one octave higher.

WE WISH YOU A MERRY CHRISTMAS

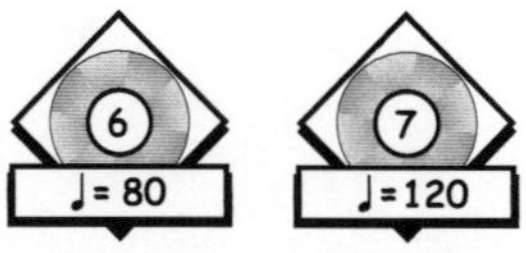

Traditional English Carol

UP ON THE HOUSETOP

Duet Accompaniment

When played as a duet, the student part is played one octave higher.

UP ON THE HOUSETOP

Words and Music by
Benjamin R. Hanby

Lively

JINGLE BELLS

Words and Music by
James S. Pierpont

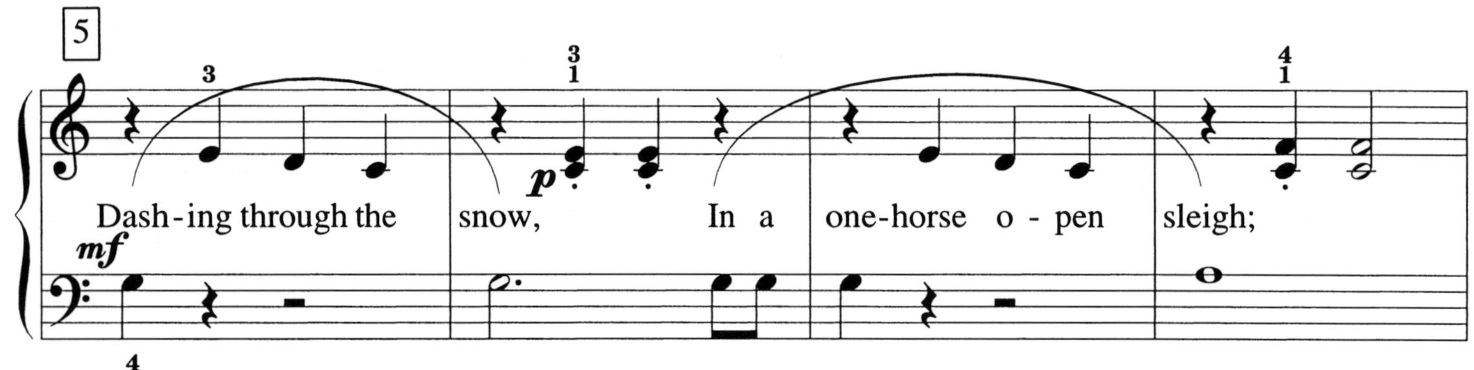

★ Loco appears after the use of an *8va* to indicate that the music should be played in the octave written.

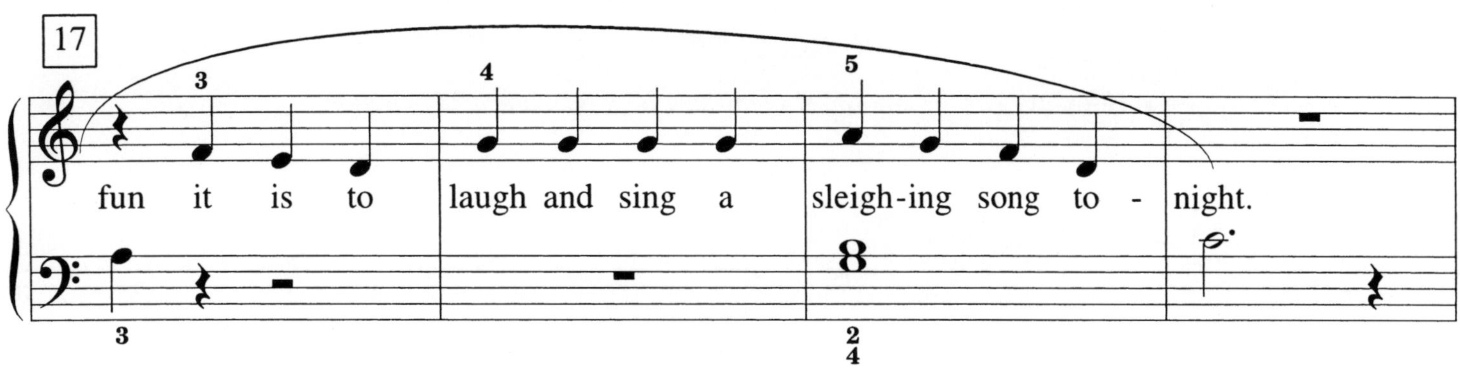
17
fun it is to laugh and sing a sleigh-ing song to - night.

21
Jin - gle bells, Jin - gle bells, Jin - gle all the

24
way! Oh, what fun it is to ride in a

27
1.
one-horse o - pen sleigh!
2.
one-horse o - pen sleigh!

GOOD KING WENCESLAS

Duet Accompaniment

When played as a duet, the student part is played one octave higher.

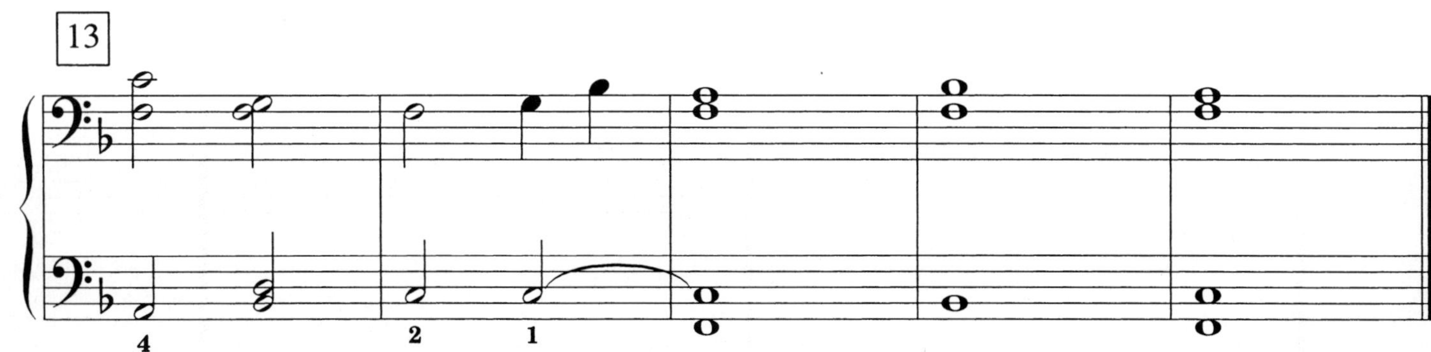

GOOD KING WENCESLAS

Words by John Mason Neale
Music from 13th Century

Moderato

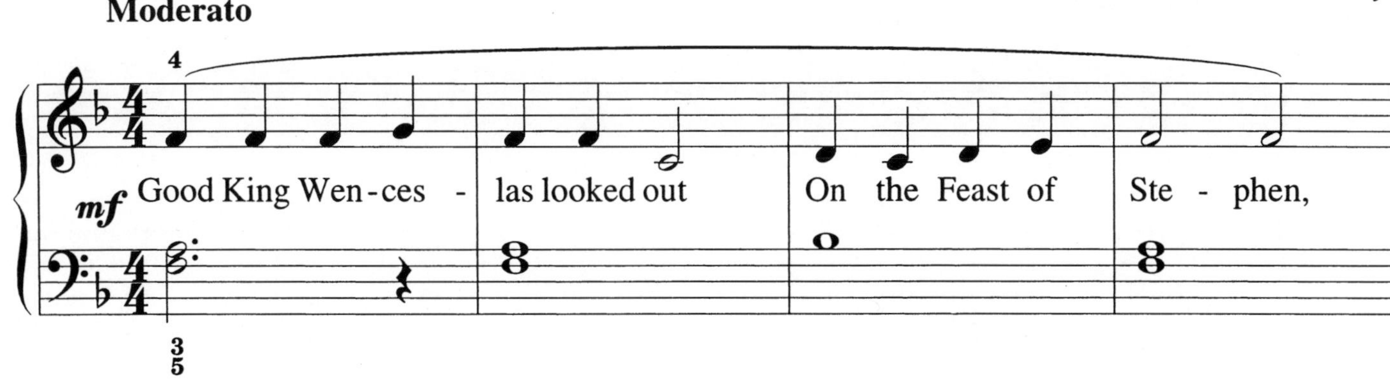

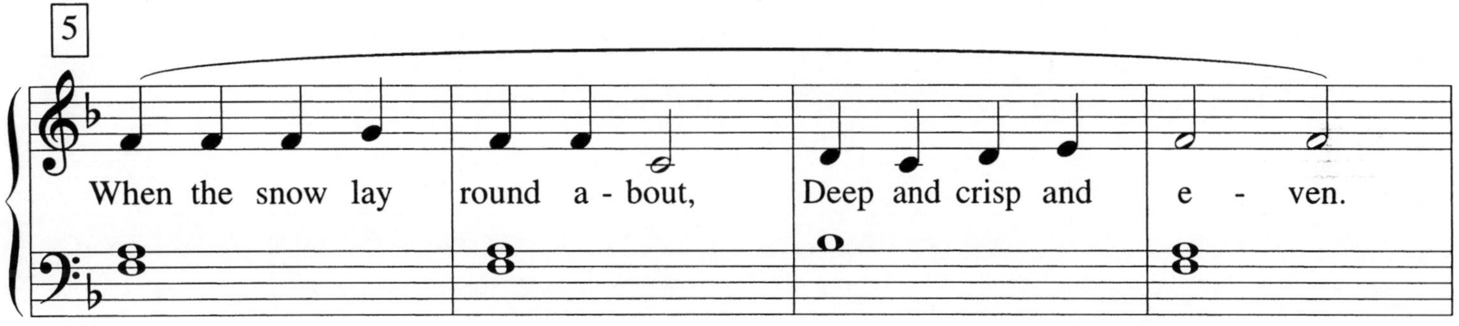

WE THREE KINGS
Duet Accompaniment

When played as a duet, the student part is played one octave higher.

WE THREE KINGS

Words and Music by
John H. Hopkins, Jr.

Moderately

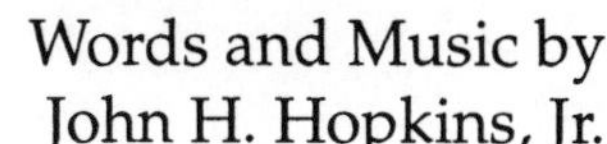

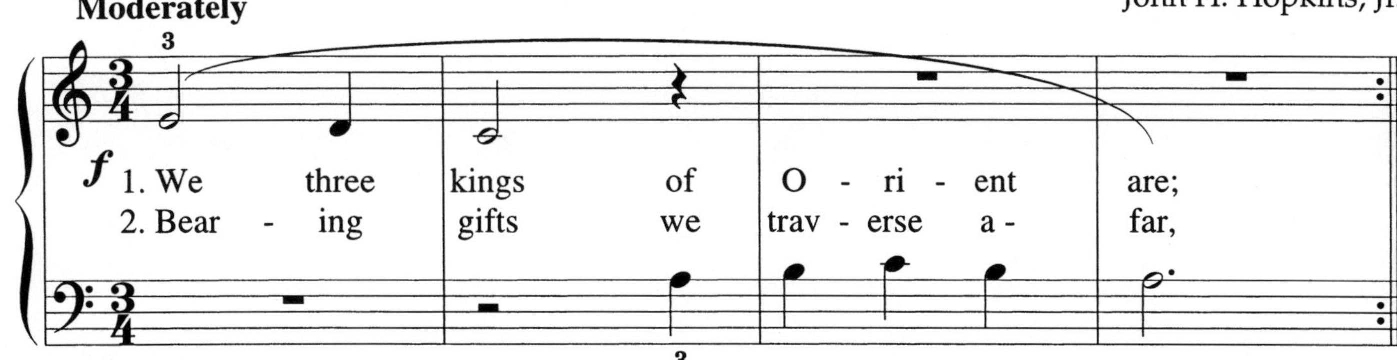

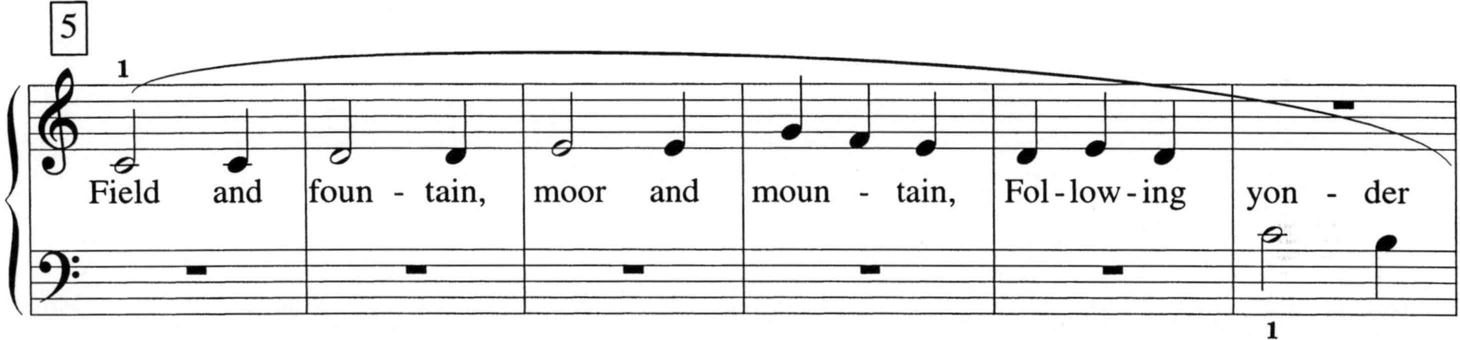

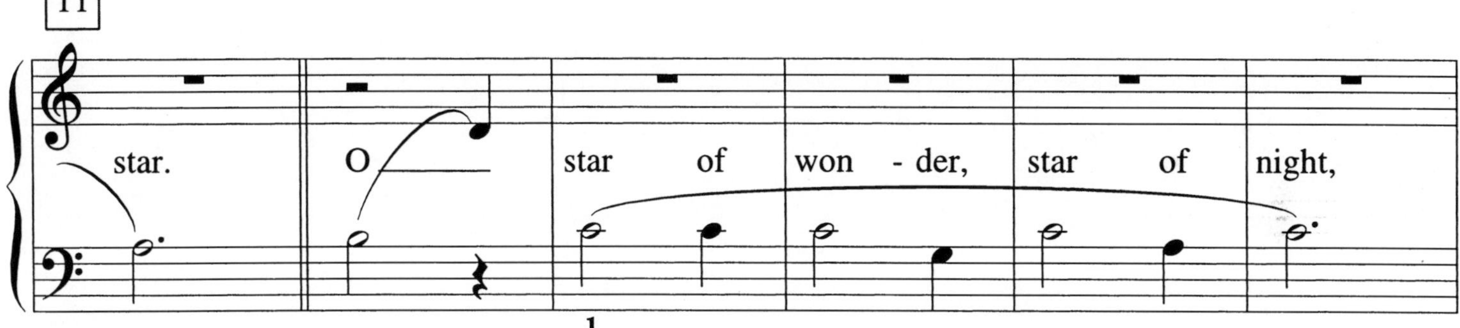

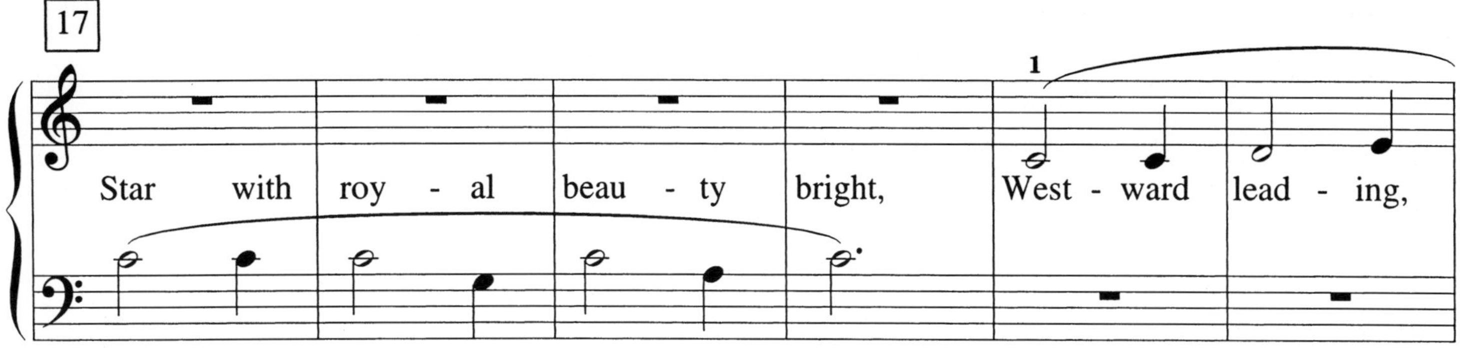

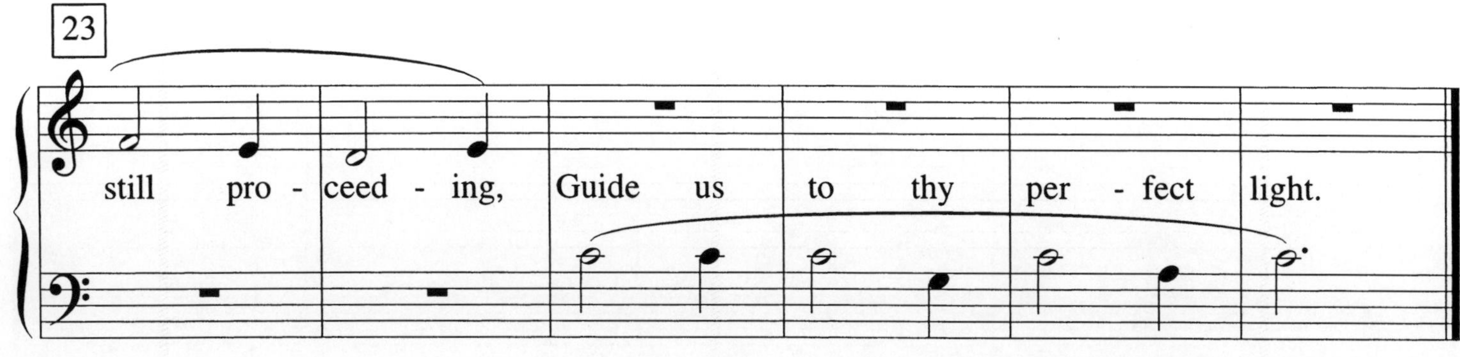

OH COME, ALL YE FAITHFUL

Duet Accompaniment

When played as a duet, the student part is played one octave higher.

OH COME, ALL YE FAITHFUL

Words and Music by
John Francis Wade,
Translation by Frederick Oakeley

Brightly

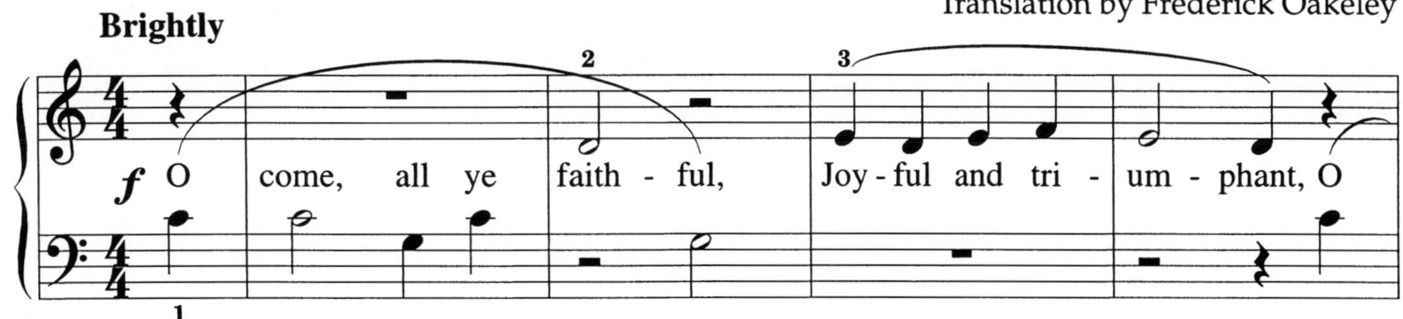

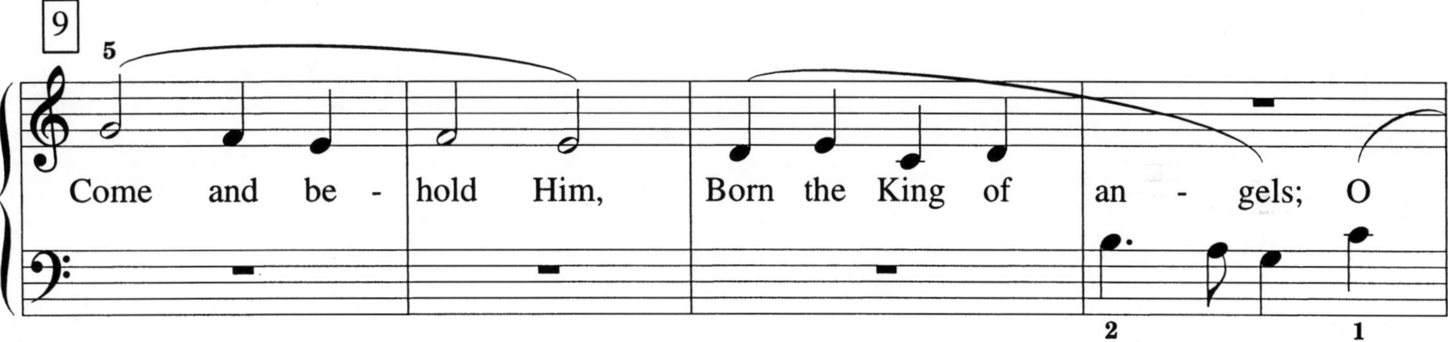

JOY TO THE WORLD
Duet Accompaniment
When played as a duet, the student part is played one octave higher.

JOY TO THE WORLD

Words by Isaac Watts
Music by George F. Handel,
Adapted by Lowell Mason

THE FIRST NOEL

Moderato

Traditional English Carol

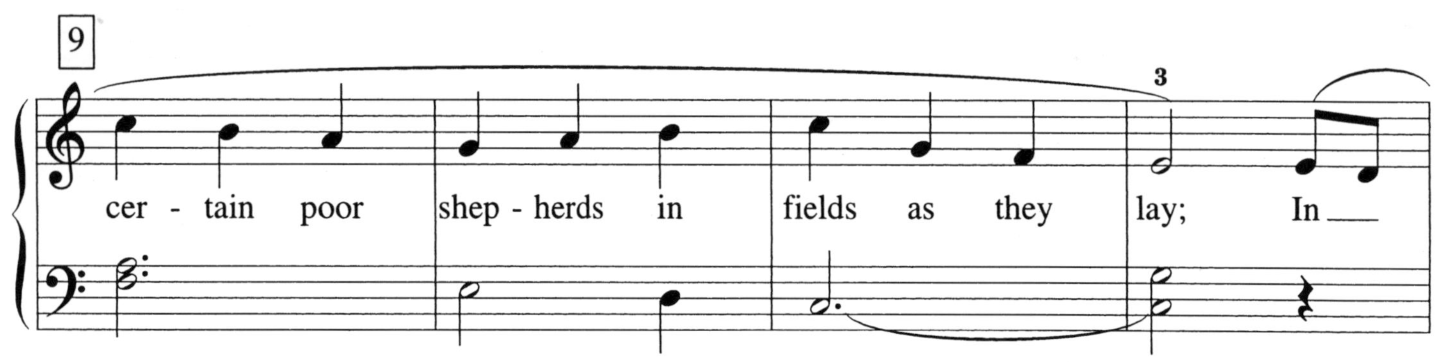

17
cold win - ter's night that was so deep.
21
No - el, No - el, No - el, No - el,
25
Born is the King of Is - ra - el!
29
pp
rit.

AWAY IN A MANGER

19th Century American Carol
Music by James Ramsey Murray

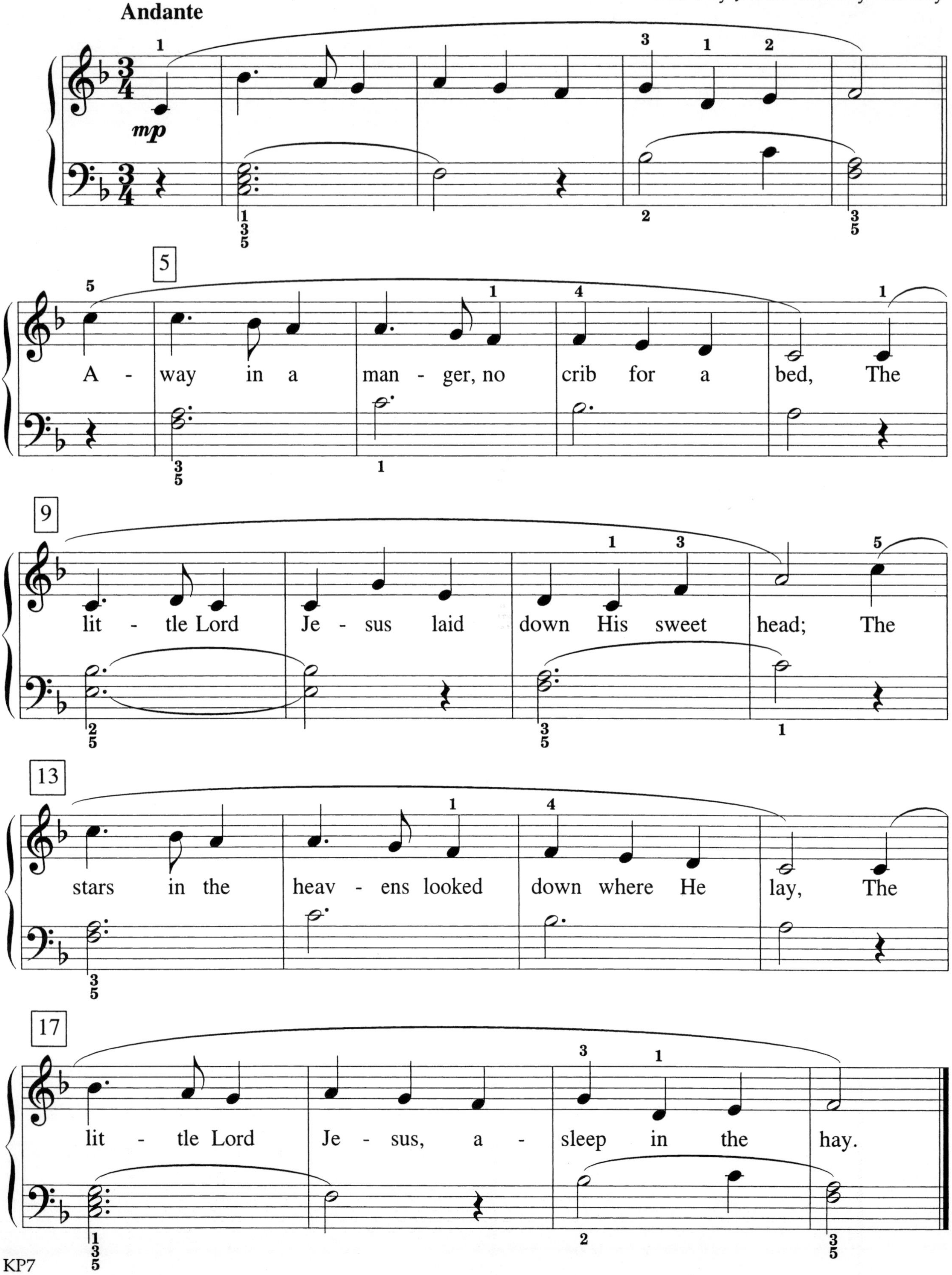

KP7

O LITTLE TOWN OF BETHLEHEM

Words by Phillips Brooks
Music by Lewis H. Redner

Andante

KP7

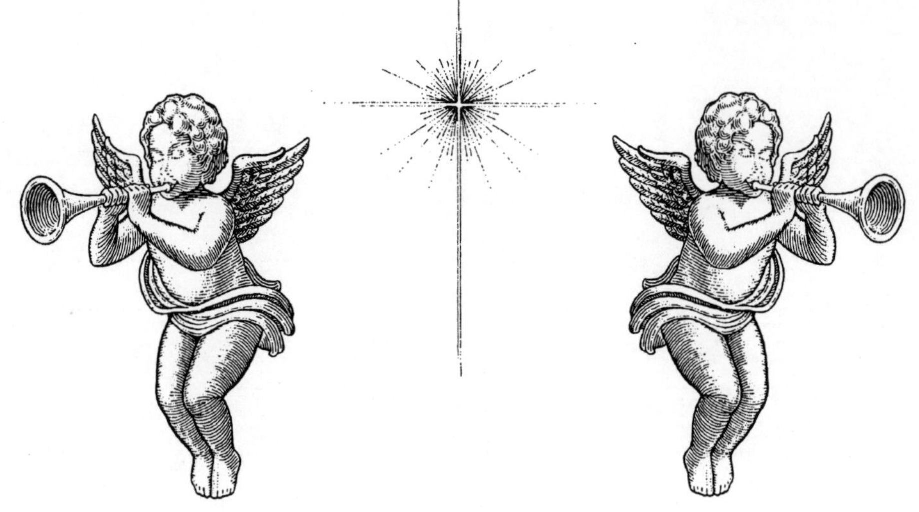

ANGELS WE HAVE HEARD ON HIGH

Traditional French Carol

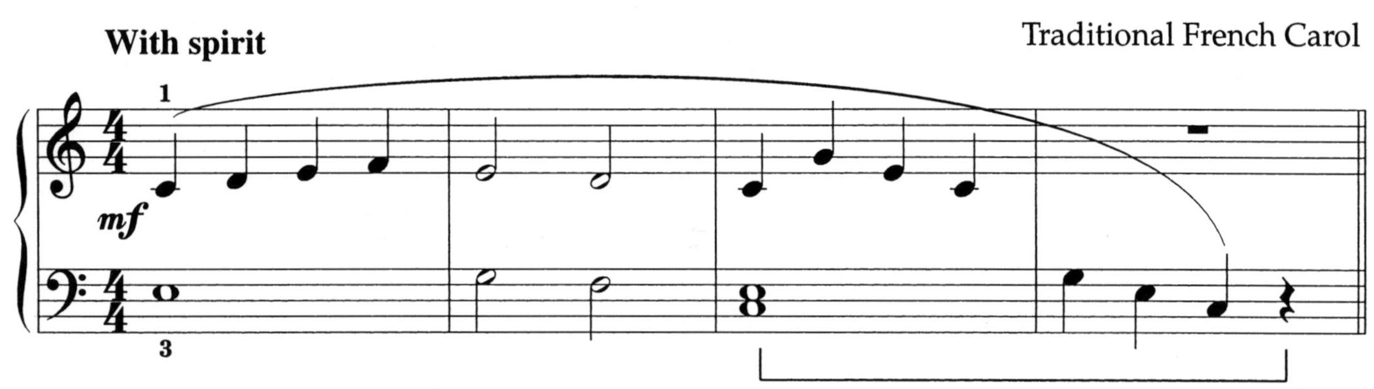

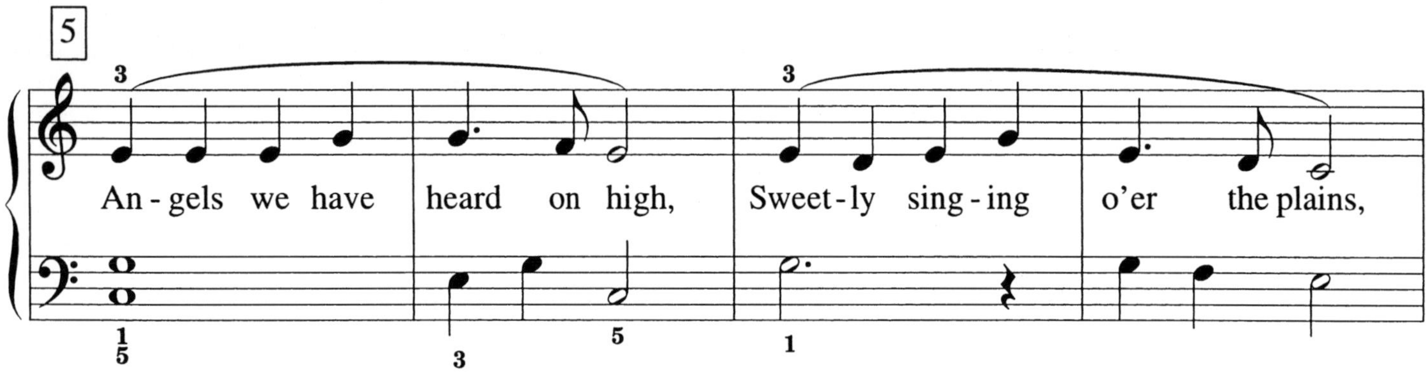

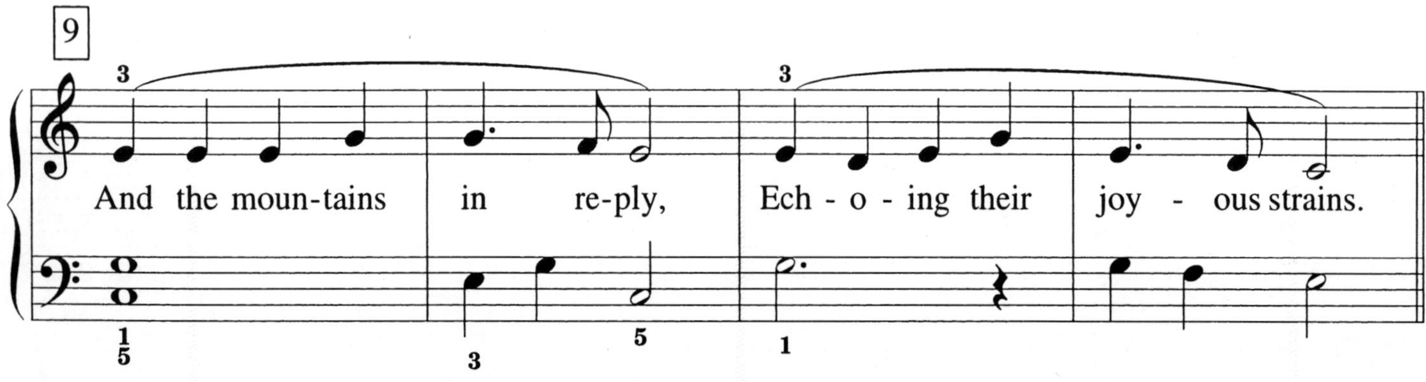

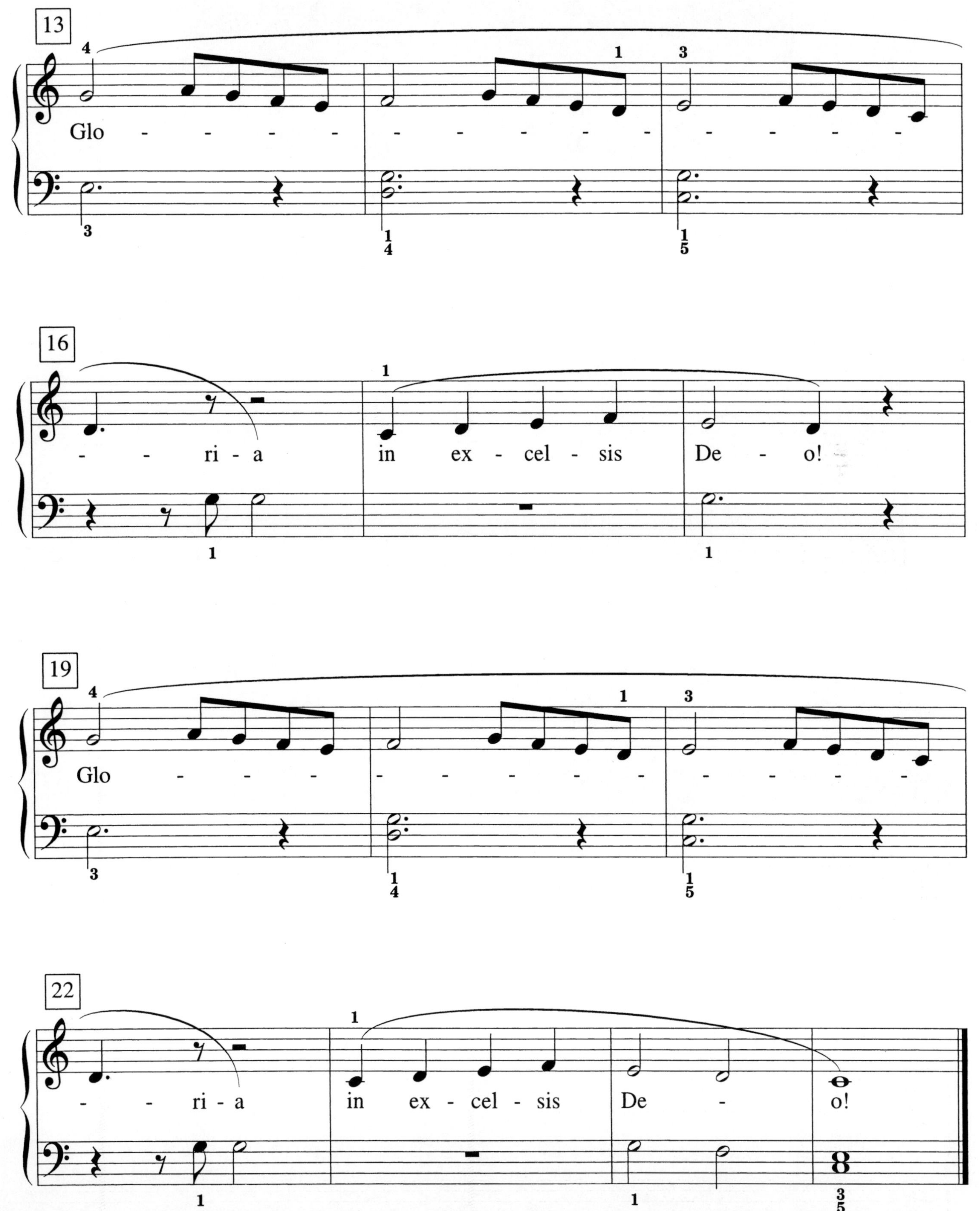

13
Glo - - - - - - - - - - - - -
16
- - ri - a in ex - cel - sis De - o!
19
Glo - - - - - - - - - - - - -
22
- - ri - a in ex - cel - sis De - o!

SILENT NIGHT

Words by Joseph Mohr
Music by Franz Gruber

Andante

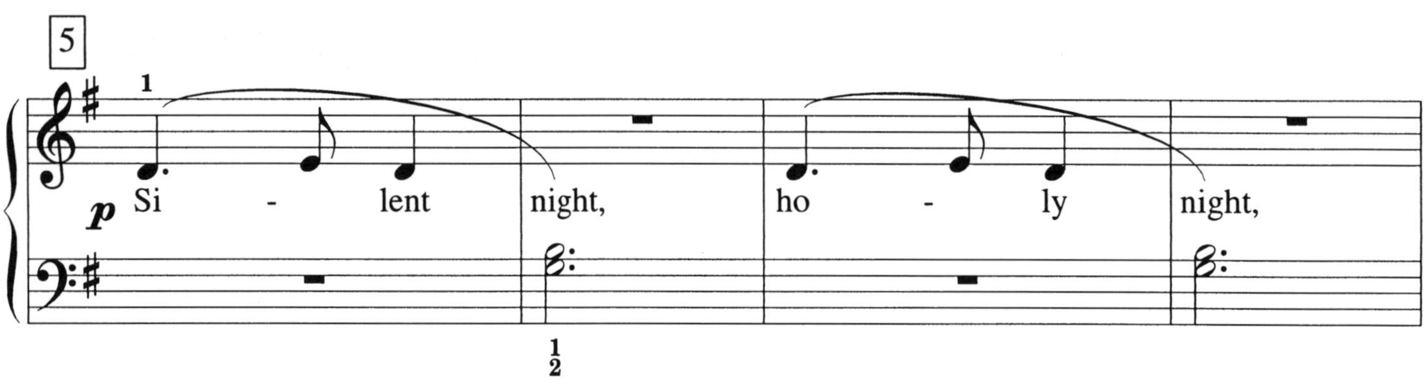

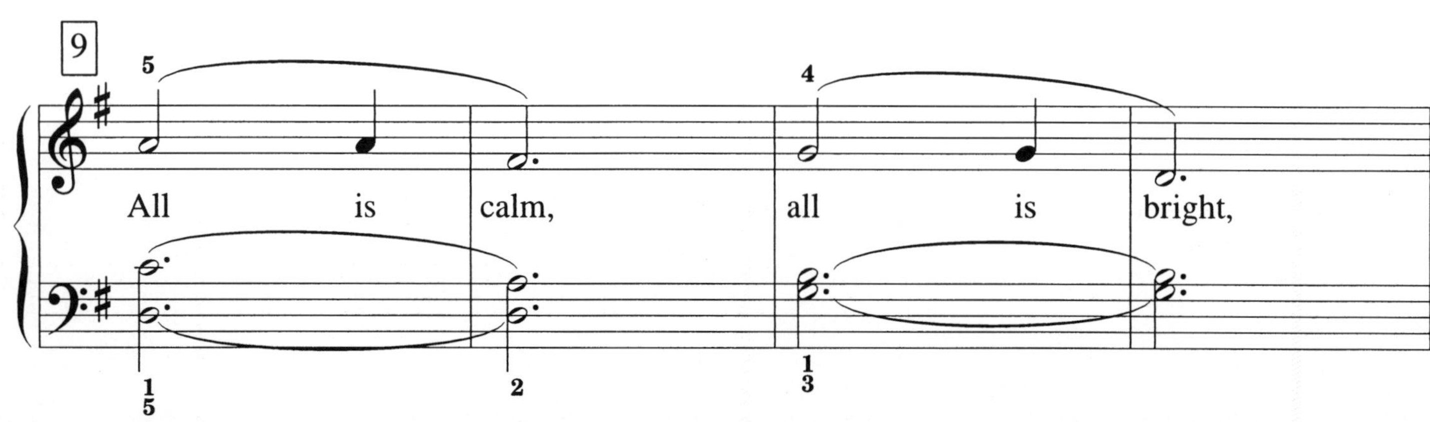

13
'Round yon Vir - gin Moth - er and Child.

17
Ho - ly In - fant so ten - der and mild,

21
Sleep in heav - en - ly peace,

25
Sleep in heav - en - ly peace.
pp rit.

HARK! THE HERALD ANGELS SING

Words by Charles Wesley
Music by Felix Mendelssohn,
Adapted by W. H. Cummings

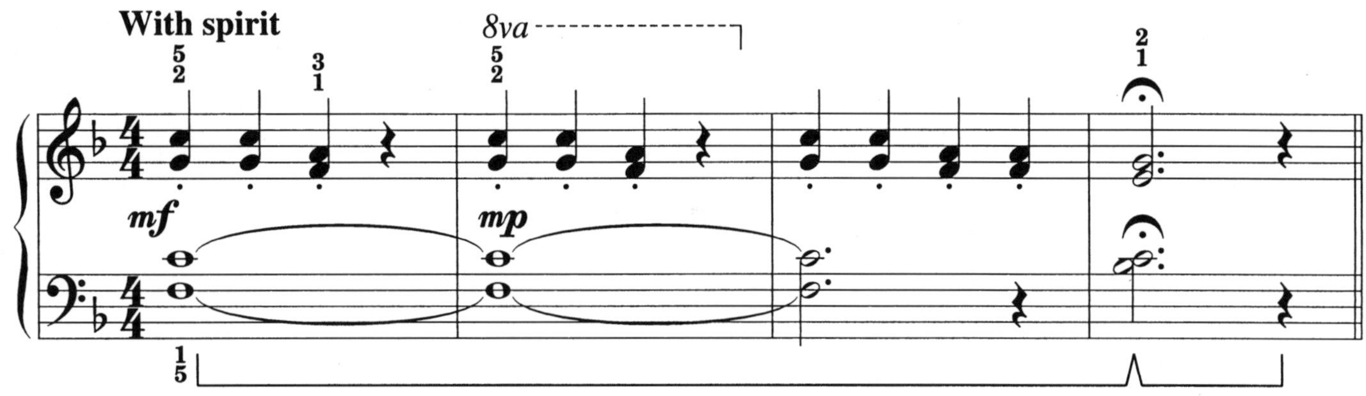

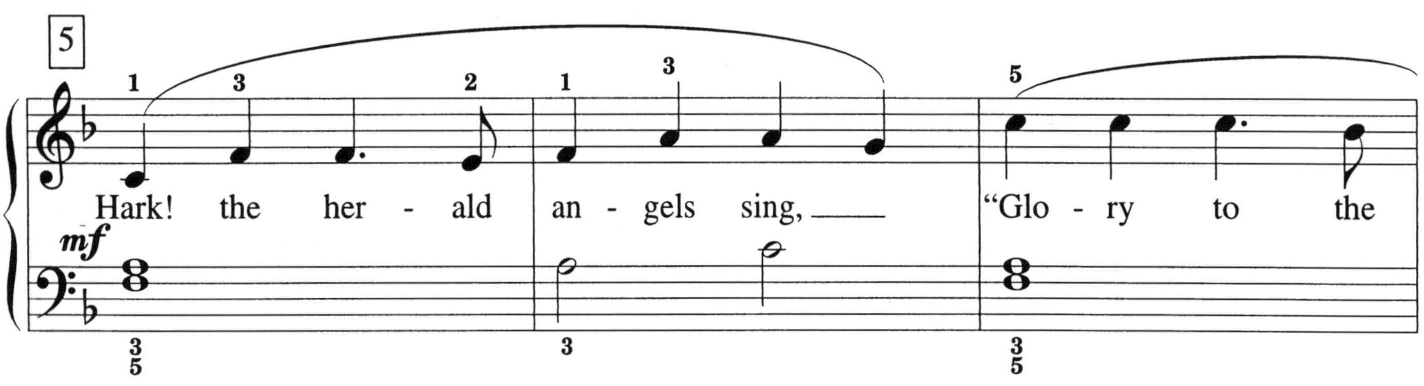

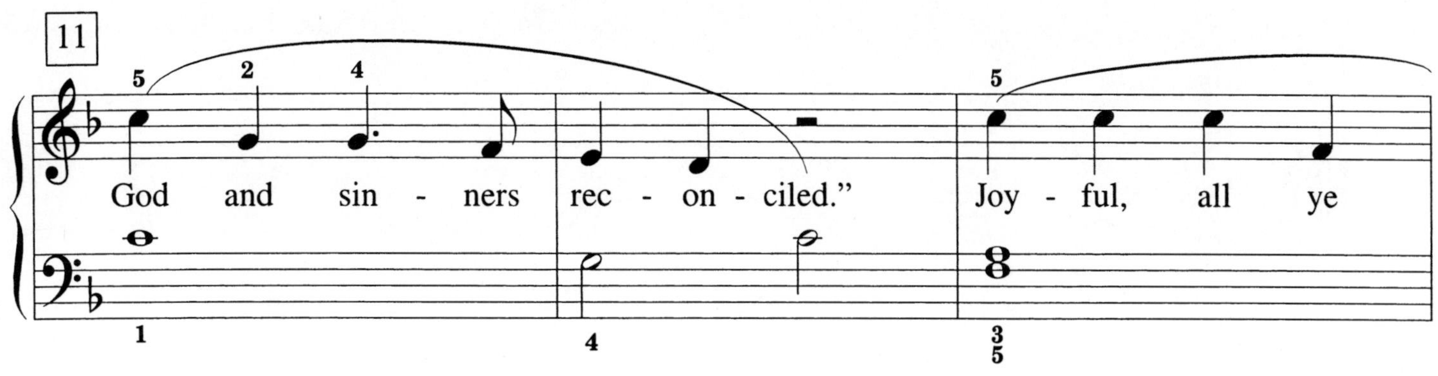
11
God and sin - ners rec - on - ciled." Joy - ful, all ye

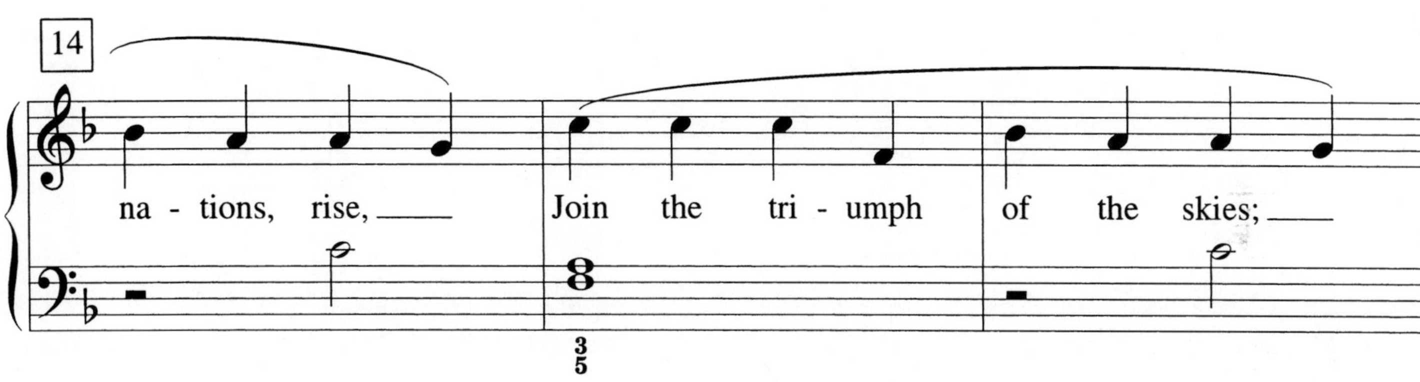
14
na - tions, rise, ___ Join the tri - umph of the skies; ___

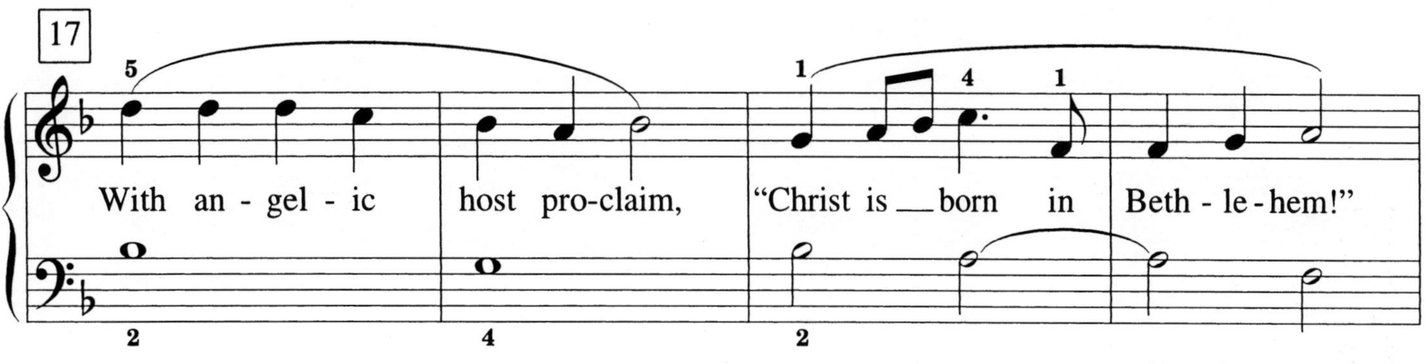
17
With an - gel - ic host pro-claim, "Christ is ___ born in Beth - le -hem!"

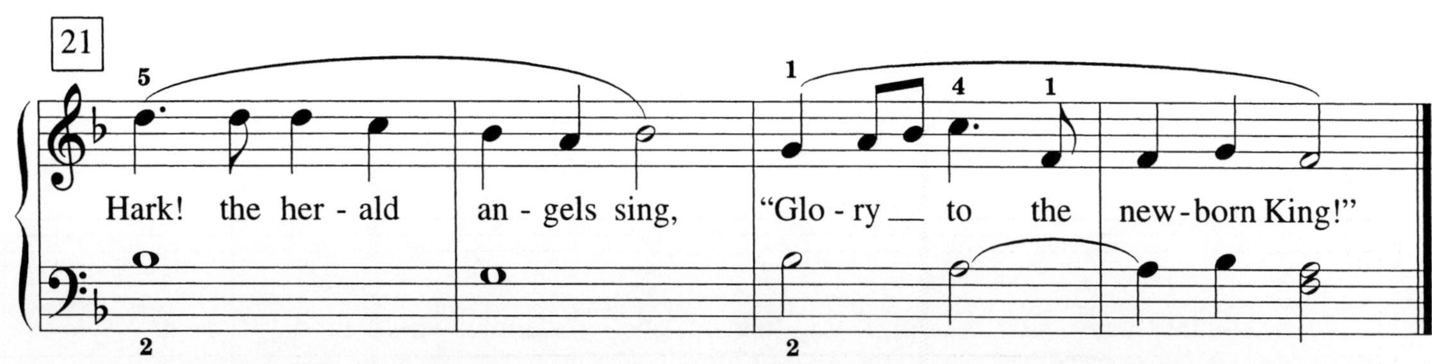
21
Hark! the her - ald an - gels sing, "Glo - ry ___ to the new -born King!"

O CHRISTMAS TREE

Traditional German Carol

DECK THE HALL

Traditional American Words
to an Old Welsh Air

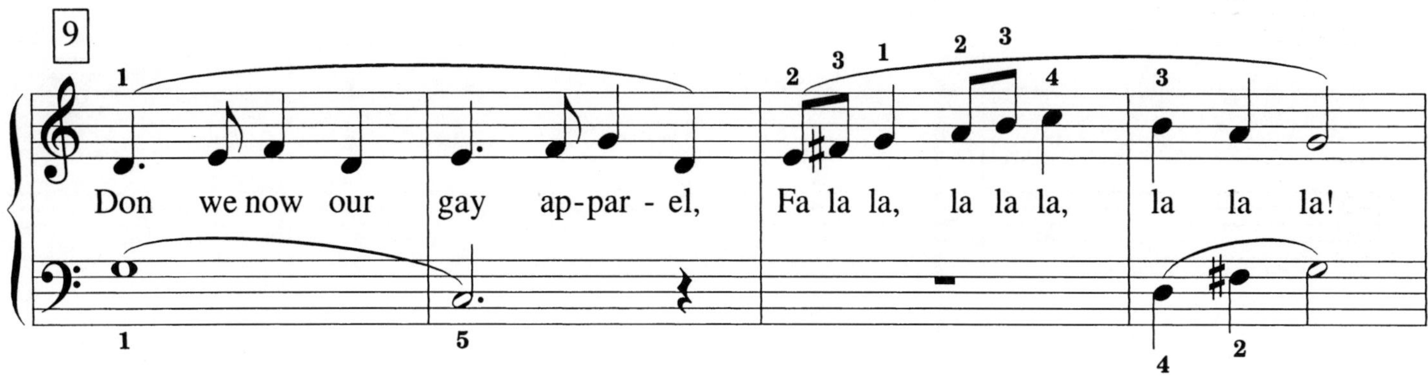

RUDOLPH THE RED-NOSED REINDEER

Words and Music by
Johnny Marks

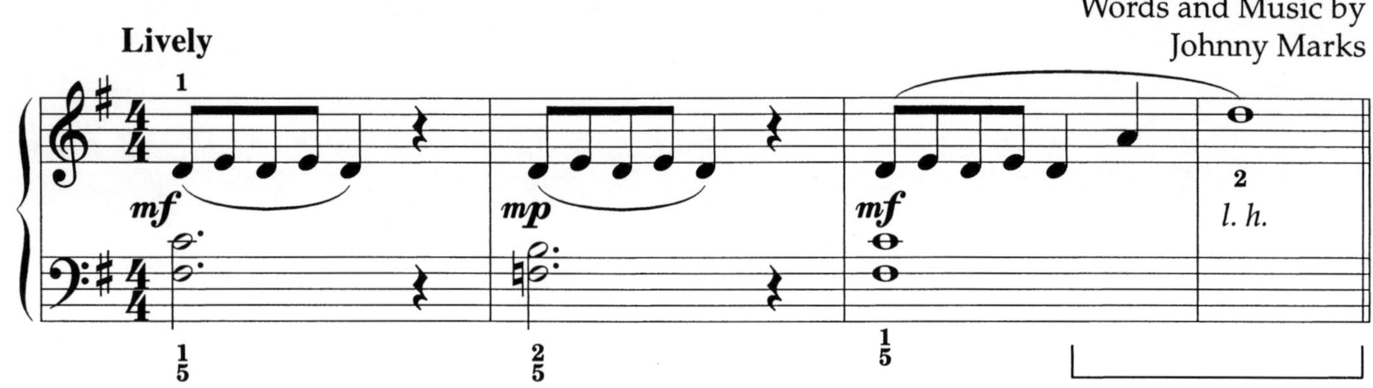

They nev - er let poor Ru-dolph join in an - y rein-deer games.
Then one fog - gy Christ-mas Eve, San - ta came to say:
"Ru-dolph, with your nose so bright, won't you guide my sleigh to-night?"
Then how the rein-deer loved him as they shout-ed out with glee:
"Ru-dolph, the red-nosed rein-deer, you'll go down in his - to - ry!"

A HOLLY JOLLY CHRISTMAS

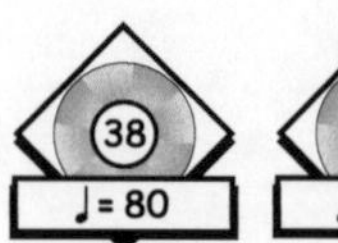

Words and Music by
Johnny Marks

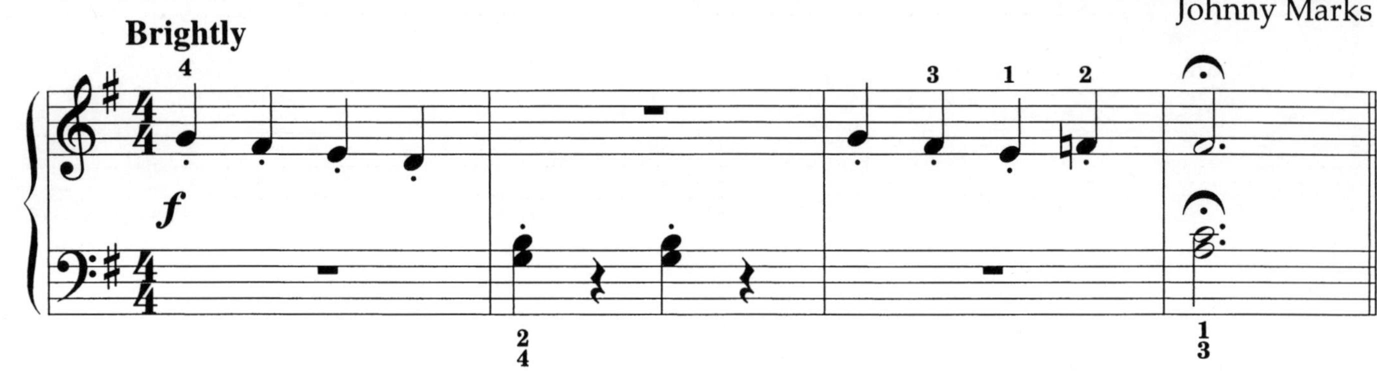

17
Say hel - lo to friends you know and ev - 'ry - one you meet. p
21
mp Oh, ho, the mis - tle - toe hung where you can see.
25
Some - bod - y waits for you, kiss her once for me. Have a
29
Hol - ly Jol - ly Christ - mas, and in case you did - n't hear
33
Oh, by gol - ly, have a Hol - ly Jol - ly Christ - mas this year.

I'LL BE HOME FOR CHRISTMAS

Words and Music by
Kim Gannon and Walter Kent

Moderately slow

© 1943 renewed 1971 Gannon and Kent Music Co.
Used with permission 1999

17
pres - ents on the tree.
21
Christ - mas Eve will find me
25
Where the love light gleams.
29
I'll be home for Christ - mas If
33
on - ly in my dreams.
rit.

I HEARD THE BELLS ON CHRISTMAS DAY

Words by Henry Wadsworth Longfellow
Music by John Baptiste Calkin

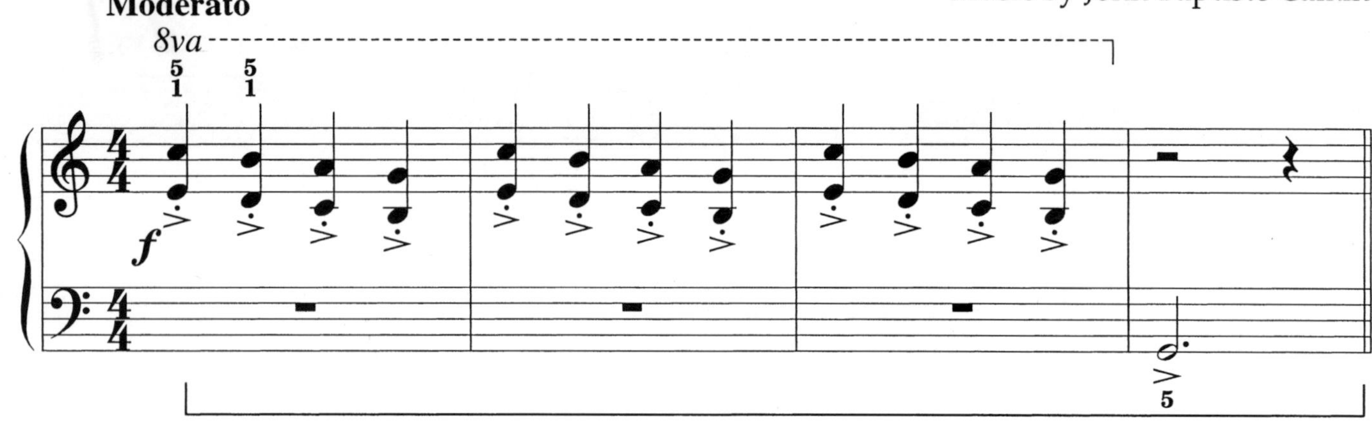

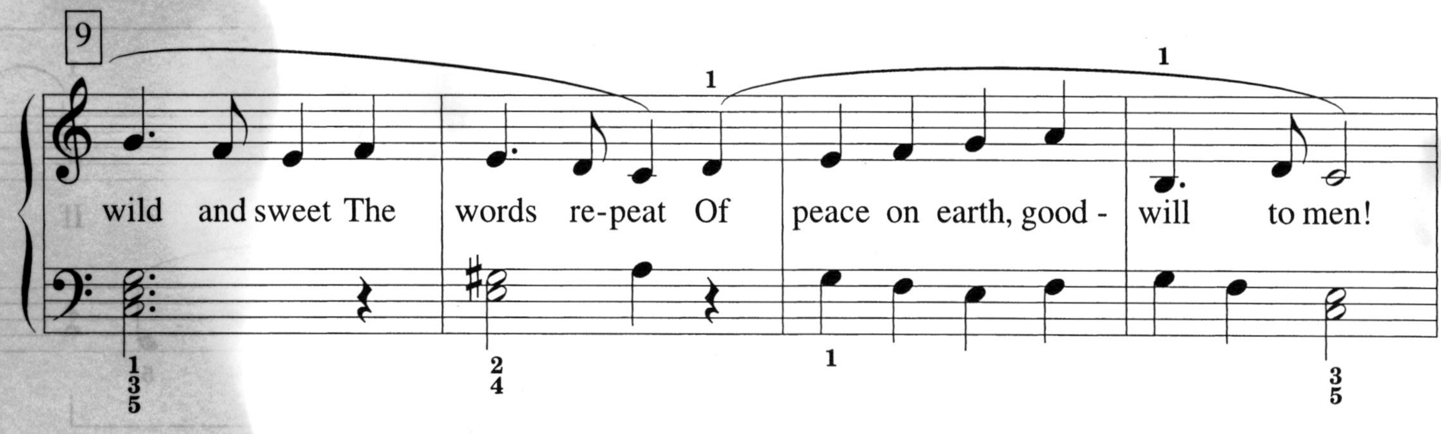

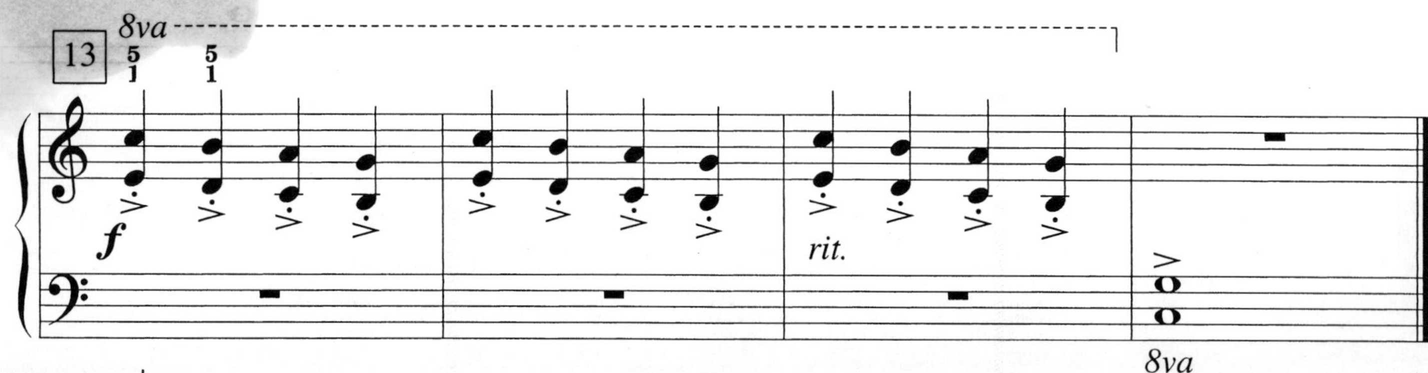